Greater Balance, Greater Reward

Five Steps to Better Health, Productivity, and Work Life Balance

Jeff Kooz

3 3158 01065 6202

ISBN: 1523875194
ISBN 13: 9781523875191
Library of Congress Control Number: 2016902642
CreateSpace Independent Publishing Platform
North Charleston, South Carolina

Download Your *Free* Audiobook and Action Guide Now.
Many readers have experienced greater success by downloading the Greater Balance Audiobook and Action Guide.
To download, visit **www.greaterbalancebook.com**.

Disclaimer

THE INFORMATION IN this book is for informational purposes only and should not substitute for professional advice where the facts and circumstances warrant. Claims made by the author may not be representative of average results or outcomes. If you require professional assistance, you should always consult your primary-care physician or other health-care provider to discuss your particular facts, circumstances, and needs.

Contents

My "Aha" Moment

IN TODAY'S FRENETIC world, it can seem like your health, productivity, and work-life balance are spinning out of control. I felt this way in the past and have spoken with countless people who feel like the harder they work, the more the things that really matter seem to fall apart.

Do you ever feel this way?

Greater Balance, Greater Reward offers a surprisingly simple way to overcome life's stubborn challenges with less stress!

Believe me, I know what it's like to live a stressful life and have little to show for it.

After being laid off three times, working nights and weekends, and watching my health deteriorate before the age of thirty ... I desperately began to look for a better path. Like many people, I immersed myself in many of the pop psychology books that promise results, only to find myself constantly living a repeat episode of past failures.

Something was missing, but I wasn't sure what.

Then everything changed. Have you ever heard the saying "When the student is ready, the master appears"?

This is what happened to me. One day, while walking in a park, the answer hit me—as clear and vivid as if it had been staring at me all the time!

I saw, in my mind's eye, a picture of a new life, and from that moment forward, this new life actually became my reality. Within a few months, I lost fifty pounds, and I have kept it off for over ten years with ease. Losing excess weight also helped me reduce stress, fatigue, and frustration, which were infecting my work and personal relationships.

People immediately noticed a difference and asked me what happened.

I tried explaining my vision in the park, but nobody could figure out what I was talking about. Eventually I quit trying. I assumed that I was just "lucky." Somehow, some way, I had managed to "offload" problems and live a much more carefree, productive life. I just couldn't explain how.

Thankfully, I had another "aha" moment—the realization that my transformation originated from five specific steps anyone can take to dissolve inner resistance to change!

And, to bring this system to life, I wrote an endearing story about a young professional who learns the "five step process" through an enigmatic man at a local café.

When I shared this allegory with family and friends—they were able to discover the same magical secret that I experienced over ten years ago.

Are you ready to discover this secret, too?

If you're feeling burned out and ready for lasting change, don't walk away from this book. The story is short and engaging; you can probably read it in one sitting.

More importantly, this book reveals a powerful problem-solving system you can put to use right away! You'll discover:

- The secret to uncovering hidden beliefs that may be the real cause of excess weight, stress, or a lack of productivity.
- The surprising five-steps that reverse these problems naturally—just by leveraging the universal power of balance.

- How to dramatically increase your creative problem-solving skills by replacing time-based goals with timeless vision.

As you put these steps into action, you can experience the same results I'm *still* enjoying today: better health, productivity, and work-life balance!

So grab a comfortable seat and enjoy the fictional narrative that follows. After the story, we'll review some of the most important aspects of balance and how you can harness them for your own "aha" moment!

1

RAY'S FINGERS WERE numb as he fumbled for loose change in his pocket. He'd been coming to the neighborhood café for years, and he still never remembered to bring enough cash.

"I'll take the usual," he mumbled as the girl across from him extended a mug. His legs felt like massive tree trunks as he shuffled to the coffee dispenser.

"Ah." He breathed a sigh of relief as the hot liquid gushed into his cup. Its rich aroma triggered sweeter memories of a more carefree past.

He could picture his grandmother humming as she gingerly tossed pancakes on the griddle. She would bring a fresh cup of coffee to Ray's grandfather, who had disappeared behind his morning paper.

Ray indulged the flashbacks until a sudden splash of coffee soaked his knuckles and sent a twinge of pain down his spine.

"Curse it!" Ray shouted, jerking the cup toward his chest and sloshing his beverage all over the counter. He moaned in disgust as a server wiped the spill with a soiled rag.

Somewhere in the back of the room he heard a familiar laugh. He'd seen a cute brunette a few times lately at the café, always sitting in the same spot with some old man. She was back, and so was he.

Ray's eyes unconsciously did somersaults when he thought about the pair. For some reason, the old guy had amassed a cult following. People had been pouring into the café for years to see him.

The cycle was so predictable that it bordered on pathetic. People of all types came to the café just to meet with the enigmatic man. Ray figured he must be some kind of psychologist; at times, much to his dismay, Ray overheard conversations during which people dumped all their woes on the table for the old man to sort out.

What was particularly odd was the way these people seemed to change over time. Many appeared as rumpled as Ray at first, but after several months, they underwent an unequivocal metamorphosis.

As soon as it happened, the acolytes disappeared. In their place, fresh followers came in.

Ray was dying to find out what was going on. Was this man a guru? Maybe it was a more sinister situation. Perhaps he was a charlatan, pretending to befriend troubled souls and then swindling them out of their life savings.

Ray slowly stirred a third packet of sugar into his coffee. As he stared into the cup, old, familiar problems began to surface in his mind.

Relationships, primarily broken, wafted through his mind's eye like a trail of dark cigar smoke. He sighed as his thoughts meandered to the imminent disaster with Jenny, his fiancée.

At first their relationship had been healthy. However, after countless disagreements and strained feelings, they both knew it was only a matter of time before they would have to part ways.

His career was equally defunct. Ray had worked at his company for twenty years with only one promotion. Even though he had strong credentials, he couldn't get along with others. Therefore, he had been quarantined to work on "special projects."

Despite all this, his health problems irked him the most. He was in the prime of his life, yet he felt like an old man.

It wasn't like he hadn't tried to improve his health. In fact, he had joined almost every gym in town and even employed a personal trainer. Ray chuckled when he recalled this character. His name was Biff, and he must have been a rampant sociopath.

Biff used to take Ray outside and make him run laps around the complex. After a minute or two, Ray's sides would begin to ache, and he would crumple over in pain. Biff's solution to the issue would be to shove Ray on the ground and scream, demanding that he do push-ups like a "real man."

It was too much, and Ray left the harsh world of exercise for more sanguine alternatives. He tried everything he read or heard about. He cut calories, carbohydrates, and even his favorite cereal, which was his personal epitome of sacrifice.

Nothing worked for long. Like many people, he just wasn't cut out for healthy diets. He tried supplements, and they didn't work. He even tried acupuncture, meditation, and hypnosis.

In the end he reached a daunting conclusion: being trim and healthy was for others.

The negative effects of this conclusion were far-reaching. He suffered from high cholesterol and high blood pressure. The doctor also said he was treading a dangerous tightrope with blood sugar. He would be diabetic in a matter of months if he didn't curb his insatiable appetite for sweets.

Life seemed so unfair. He couldn't sleep well anymore, and he ached every time he moved. His knees seemed to be buckling, and his lower back felt like an elephant had stomped on it.

Ray blinked, waking from his soul-searching, and saw the pretty brunette stand and hug the old man. Then she bounced toward the exit. Ray simply couldn't stand it any longer; he had to gather some reconnaissance. What was going on?

With uncharacteristic directness, Ray motioned his hand and caught the lady's attention.

"Yes?" she said as she made an abrupt U-turn. Her eyes were wide with a rapt attention that Ray found slightly intimidating.

He looked down, self-conscious. Stammering, he tried to bring himself to ask her who that man was. The words clung to the roof of his mouth like caramel.

Her brow furrowed, and she tried to decipher what this pear-shaped guy with pink cheeks was saying.

"Are you asking me who that man is over there?" She pointed to the back of the café.

Ray nodded briskly. "Yes. Who is that guy, anyway? What are you and others doing with him?"

He said it. It felt like an albatross finally slid off his back. Maybe he could finally solve a mystery that had eluded him for years.

Unfortunately, the vivacious lady—Nancy, it turns out—burst into a far-fetched story that Ray found completely unintelligible. He managed to gather that the man was a retired attorney who espoused some kind of philosophy of the mind. Glancing quickly at her watch, she apologized and bolted out the door.

"He's an attorney?" Ray whispered under his breath. Now he was even more confused.

Maybe he was counseling people on legal matters. Of course, people don't always erupt into bursts of joy after meeting with attorneys.

Then he recalled something Nancy had said about philosophy. *What could that mean?*

He rubbed his forehead anxiously, almost as if he could kneed his scalp into producing an answer.

He realized that there was only one way to find out. Pressing his hands against the seat, he hoisted himself up and took one step toward the mysterious man.

Ray's life was about to change in a way he never expected.

2

AS RAY APPROACHED the man's table, he was surprised by how different the man appeared up close.

The old man, who appeared to be in his early seventies, sat quietly with his hands folded on the table. Ray shook his head and wondered if he had somehow missed the "real" guru. Was this really the man so many people flocked to see?

Ray timidly put out his hand for the man to shake. Behind the demure nature, he was masking nothing short of sheer terror. He wasn't comfortable meeting new people, much less someone so puzzling.

The man shook Ray's hand vigorously and said his name was Cal. Ray was immediately struck by something unusual about the man.

As short and small as he was, Cal emanated an unmistakable presence through the intensity in his eyes.

Almost immediately, Ray became Cal's entire focal point. Cal's steely blue eyes bored into Ray and locked him into a trance. Ray wasn't used to being the focus of someone's entire attention, but now it had happened twice in just a few minutes.

In one respect, it was affirming. Ray felt as if he was the single most important person in the world. Then again, it made him feel claustrophobic. It was kind of like being observed under a microscope.

Ray snapped out of it and asked Cal what was going on here in the back of the café. The man responded with translucent honesty. He wasn't a psychologist. As the woman had said, he was a retired attorney.

Several years ago, he had struck up an informal conversation with a lady in the café, and it led to a remarkable transformation in her life.

She, in turn, had told a friend about Cal, who came to see him, and the same phenomenon occurred. Friends told other friends, and before long, Cal had a steady following.

He didn't charge anyone for his advice and made it clear that he had no training or background in counseling.

His only objective was to share something that someone once shared with him when he was on the verge of losing everything. This gripped Ray with curiosity, and he asked what had happened.

Cal explained that he was once an aspiring attorney with a young family, and he started making sacrifices to advance his career. He strove to be the youngest partner and showed atypical promise for someone so young.

Unaware of the risks he was taking, he ended up on a landslide, sacrificing his health, relationships, and even the quality of his precious job.

One evening he sat on a park bench, drenched with rain, contemplating the nightmare that had become his new reality. His mind raced with fear as he thought about the prospect of divorce and bankruptcy. He was also certain that he would lose his job.

In just a few short years, he went from the golden boy at the firm to a burned-out shell of his former self. His body had aged ten years or more, and he often felt pressure mounting in his chest.

Just then an old lady strolled by, walking her dog. He thought it was strange that someone so elderly would be out on such a frigid evening. The air was damp and cold. He looked closer, squinting through the mist, but didn't recognize her.

She stopped and struck up a conversation. Her breath faded into the air when she spoke.

This was the last moment Cal felt like having a friendly chat. When he opened his mouth, he was afraid something nasty might slip out.

To his amazement, he began sobbing uncontrollably. Normally he could suppress the pain, but that night, he had lost all control.

As he gulped down some of his tears, words dribbled out in all their unfiltered shame. The lady stood motionless, like a phantom, while her dog whined and huddled under the freezing rain.

Before she left, she gave Cal the most peculiar advice.

He never saw her again and often wondered if he had fallen into a dream or had passed out. Maybe she was an angel sent to rescue him in his darkest hour. Regardless, the simplicity of what she said sliced through his turmoil effortlessly.

In an instant, he saw a problem that he never knew he had. It was the root of all his problems. In his mind's eye, he saw it, metaphorically, like a tablecloth. Then he saw someone yanking the cloth off the table, sending glasses and silverware splattering all over the floor.

His problem was like that cloth. It was the force that sucked everything in his life into one spiraling vortex below.

Alongside the problem he saw the solution. In fact, in seeing the problem he saw the solution automatically. Analogous to a coin, the solution was the flip side of the problem. He knew what he needed to do, starting that very moment.

When he returned home, it was as if a part of him had passed away, and a new being had been born. He really was a new person. The old identity he clung to, which was snuffing out his life, crumbled that evening. It was replaced by a fresh new way of looking at the world.

Within months, Cal's marriage was salvaged, and he began cultivating a relationship with his children that previously would have been impossible. He took practical steps to improve his health, and almost immediately there was a positive change.

Even the monsoon he was drowning under at work lifted, and he began to repair broken relationships. The old, familiar quality of his work reemerged.

People asked him what had happened; how had he experienced such a visible transformation?

At first, he told them about the encounter with the old lady; few people grasped its significance. The whole scenario seemed mystical but largely impractical.

As a result, he quit speaking about the freak encounter. Instead, he shared only some of the basic insights hidden in the lady's cryptic words. People could relate to those, but it seemed like the essence of what she communicated became lost in translation.

The practical approaches that Cal took seemed to operate best when they were coupled with the experience he'd had that evening.

Eventually, he decided he could not explain it; he had been given a gift. Regretfully, he did not know how to give that gift to someone else.

That changed one day when he met Molly.

3

MOLLY WAS A young nurse with a heart of gold but the bedside manner of a steamroller. Cal used to overhear her mobile-phone conversations at the café and had winced with empathy for whoever was on the other end of the line.

Eventually, he struck up a conversation with her, and before Cal knew what was happening, she bulldozed directly into all the dark details of her life.

For some reason, Cal had begun to have this effect on others. Strangers felt instantly comfortable with him and granted him liberal doses of implicit trust.

Cal had to repress a smile as he listened to Molly because many of her troubles mirrored his own troubles from thirty years earlier. She described herself as a "competitive perfectionist" who was fast moving and demanding. In her zealousness, she began burning bridges with nurses and doctors.

Beneath her explosive veneer, Cal could sense a kind and wounded soul. So he started asking questions. Before long, he could see how her life had begun to drift out of orbit.

Over the next two months, Cal managed to share some of the insights he received from the mysterious woman in the park. It wasn't easy at first, because he had to deconstruct what happened to him in a way that made sense to Molly.

After a number of detours, she began grasping what Cal was trying to share and experienced some major breakthroughs. She brought her life back into balance and witnessed profound improvements in her relationships, health, and career.

Ecstatic, she told others about this gentle guru, and many came to share their problems with him. In every case, he took them back to that dreary night he sat in the rain.

Then, he walked them through the simple yet profound words that old lady had uttered.

Thanks to Molly, he was also able to guide people through a step-by-step process that was actionable.

Ray heard enough. He wanted to find out what this miraculous process was. To his chagrin, Cal said that each person has to be "ready" to hear it or the words will seem empty and powerless.

He admitted that not everyone found solace in what he shared. Many left and never returned. In some cases, it wasn't applicable.

Yet this wasn't *always* the case. Often, whenever someone faithfully applied themselves to the teaching, he or she experienced significant change.

Cal invited Ray to fully share all his challenges. He said he couldn't promise results, but he would listen. If he could help, he would certainly do his best.

Once again Ray felt a chill descend down his spine as his eyes met the clear intensity of Cal's gaze. The world around them seemed to dissipate, as if he and this unusual man were the last two people on the planet.

Scratching a sudden itch on the tip of his nose, Ray gulped and started talking. He barely breathed for the next five minutes, pouring out the ghastly details of his every struggle. He recounted the relationships that ended up as the equivalent of compost and the chaos of his health and his career.

When he finished talking, his heart was pounding as if he had just run a five-minute mile.

He sat back in the chair and adjusted his neck. Cal cringed at the sound of bones snapping in rapid sequence.

In the hour that followed, Cal explained something that was so familiar, yet it was one of the strangest perspectives Ray had ever heard in his life.

4

CAL ADMITTED THAT he couldn't recall the words the lady had spoken verbatim. That evening was so emotionally charged that it seemed like a dream. However, as she spoke, a vision sprang into view. He saw a scale, and one side was out of balance with the other side.

As the lady spoke, a new life beckoned that was the polar opposite of the one he was living. It was a life of balance. Cal then actually watched the scale, in his mind's eye, move toward a state of balance.

He was given a vision of balance, and it carried him over every obstacle he faced and created nothing short of a new life.

Balance, Cal suggested, is one of the most misunderstood principles in the world. It's something everyone gives lip service to, but so few people recognize it as an agent of power.

Cal then shared some examples of balance, which helped explain its titanic significance to our existence.

The first example he gave was the position of Earth. Its distance can be described as within the habitable zone of our sun. If the earth orbited too far from the sun, the oceans would freeze. If it orbited too close, the oceans would boil. Fortunately for us, Earth's distance from the Sun is perfectly balanced between these extremes.

Cal's favorite example of balance was law. As an attorney, he lived in a world of rules and regulations. Unsurprisingly, he began to curate the idea of a "lawful universe." In his mind, he visualized a reality where systems followed intelligent rules.

Over time, as he worked with people in the café, he coined the phrase "intelligent systems."

For example, health is an intelligent system. It operates on certain patterns, and once you know those patterns, you can adjust your behavior around them.

Relationships, he explained, are also complex social systems that function best under specific guidelines. When you understand these rules, you can adjust your behavior around them to relate better with others.

Many other facets of life operate as intelligent systems, including financial, political, and, of course, physical laws. In truth, Cal explained, *everything* is governed by some system, whether we are aware of it or not.

Ray began fidgeting in his chair, so Cal quickly switched gears. He wanted Ray to see how balance can be practical for our common problems, not simply a theoretical concept.

He recommended that they first apply balance to Ray's health. That would make these concepts more concrete.

"What is balance, anyway?" Cal inquired rhetorically.

He explained that, in his estimation, balance is the sweet spot between two opposing extremes. On one side is extremely unhealthy behavior. This includes severe negligence, such as insufficient nutrition, water, exercise, and sleep.

The other side is a completely different extreme. It's the antithesis of the first side, where people actually eat or exercise too much.

Ray's problem, Cal maintained, was his tendency to oscillate between both extremes, never resting in a comfortable, healthy middle ground.

Ray thought about it. Cal was right; he never did live in a state of balance. However, he thought that balance wouldn't work, or work fast enough, so he never tried it.

Almost as if he was reading Ray's mind, Cal interjected some common logic about extremes. He said that people think, on a subconscious level, that they have to go to an extreme to generate results quickly. They believe that balance is benign. Yet balance is the *most* powerful approach, provided that you have a humble spirit and are patient with results.

The problem is that extremes produce inner resistance to sustainability. In other words, you're trapped in a system where you begin disliking whatever you are doing to generate fast results.

This system provokes the subconscious mind to seek relief from stress. Unfortunately, to satisfy this relief, people often move back toward the original extreme.

The net effect is that people vacillate from one extreme to another, never finding that comfortable middle ground.

Cal emphasized that the only way around this conundrum is balance. Balance involves little or no suffering. We practice positive behaviors that we can enjoy in doses that are acceptable to our subconscious mind. The upshot is these balanced behaviors produce profoundly positive results, and these behaviors also seem effortless.

One would think that if balance offers such an incontrovertible advantage, everyone would practice it. But Cal admitted that, unfortunately, just the opposite is true. There is a strange paradox between what people consciously assert about balance and what they actually practice.

For example, if you ask about personal finance, most people recommend a balance in their portfolio assets or the ratio between spending and saving. If you ask about careers, they'll articulate the virtues of work-life balance. If you ask about health, they'll advocate balance in diet and exercise.

Amazingly, these people may not actually practice *any* of these recommendations. There is obviously a gap between people's conscious and subconscious beliefs about balance.

Cal hypothesized that culture has a great deal to do with it. He described it as a type of "cultural hypnosis."

Our culture doesn't always promote balance. Instead, we want everything instantly, and we are willing to pay a premium later. We're impatient. We want food via a drive-through within thirty seconds. We want the big house or nice car without saving for it first. We're used to accessing information instantly online or through mobile applications.

Therefore, we expect the same push-button results for everything, including health, career, and relationships. We're forever looking for the easy, fast path.

The "cultural hypnosis" Cal referred to was the fact that people aren't even aware of this perception of reality. This makes it increasingly difficult for them to escape. In essence, you can't escape from the prison you don't know exists.

As a consequence, Cal explained, achieving slow, sure results over time has become almost completely obsolete for many people. Even though we consciously say we believe in balance, we have learned to subconsciously resist it.

Ray found this interesting. He could relate. As he began to reflect on what Cal was saying, he could see that he tried putting fast patches on gaping wounds all over his life. When they didn't work, he assumed he didn't have the "right" patch. So, instead of choosing balance, he went in search of another quick fix.

Armed with this new way of seeing the world, Ray realized he needed a sure, stable path. Balance seemed like the right approach, and he wanted to take action. So he asked Cal how to begin.

To his astonishment, Cal said that it was Ray who needed to answer that question. Otherwise, the system could not work.

Moreover, the first step Cal recommended seemed positively ludicrous.

5

CAL WAS ONLY a spokesperson for balance, he said. He could not help people actually put it to work. Each person must do it for himself or herself.

Ray was crestfallen. Cal had led him to the foot of the path but now seemed to be walking away. Wasn't there some map or guide he could offer?

Cal advised Ray to follow a five-step path that he had developed over time, with the help from people in the café. Yet, he reminded Ray, it is a path Ray would have to take on his own.

He walked over to the dart board in the corner of the café and wrote each of the five steps in chalk on the board where teams could keep score:

> *Step 1: Pick an area of life you would like to improve, and see the improvement as if it is already a present reality.*
> *Step 2: Determine what balance would look like, as if it's already being practiced in this area of your life.*
> *Step 3: Pay attention to inner resistance to balance from your subconscious mind.*
> *Step 4: Reframe your thinking by questioning your own assumptions in light of objective reality.*
> *Step 5: Take just one step toward balance, and see what happens.*

Ray sank into his chair, mortified. This wasn't at all what he expected. He was hoping for something simple and amusing, and he pleaded with Cal to explain what all this meant.

Cal walked him through each of these steps, one by one, with more detail this time. He punctuated each point with a toss of a dart.

First, he said, it's critical that we are clear about the desired end state we wish to reach. The subconscious mind cannot connect with ambiguity.

Thump. A dart hit the board.

Cal used health once again as an illustration. In his personal case, he wanted to live without the excess weight he had begun to accumulate. He didn't set a goal to lose weight by a certain time. Instead, he "saw" a reality, in his mind's eye, of being trim and fit, as if it were already happening.

Cal suggested that such visualization is critical in enlisting the subconscious mind as an ally. If the mind believes in a reality, it will begin supporting it, even if that reality hasn't fully manifested.

Second, balance means looking at the reality, and the behaviors that produce it, as a single entity. They are interconnected. Cal knew that balanced diet, activity, and sleep were essential to the reality he wanted to experience.

Thump. Another dart, this one just inside the first.

Third, Cal recognized that he might sense inner resistance from the subconscious mind. Because of our "need-it-now" culture, our inner mind would prefer taking a faster, more extreme path over the slow and steady path of balance.

Thump. Cal was surprisingly steady at darts, and Ray could at least see where his tosses were headed, if not his philosophy.

From a detached state, Cal could feel objections bubbling up inside him:

It will never work.
Balance is boring.
I can get what I want faster by extreme measures.

Fourth, he looked at those objections with a dispassionate critical eye. When he managed to separate himself from these thoughts, he could see that they were illusions.

Thump. A dart hit just inside the outer ring of the bull's-eye.

Balance *does* work, and it isn't necessarily boring, Cal told him. It may be true that extreme measures can produce results faster, but these carry a cost. The worst is usually eventual failure.

And then, on the dartboard, a miss. Cal shrugged and smiled.

When we succeed through extremes, we typically end up returning to old behaviors just as quickly. Before long, we inhabit the same reality that extremes promised to liberate us from.

For Cal, balance translated to activities he enjoyed, like walking and golf, and yes, he'd been in more than his share of dart leagues over the years.

It also involved eating a little less while eating higher-quality foods, particularly vegetables, healthy oils, nuts, and berries. These foods helped his body become healthier while eradicating uncontrollable cravings and food addictions. Additionally, he drank more water and enjoyed more rest and relaxation.

What happened?

Cal not only lost excess weight but also enjoyed the behaviors themselves. They were not a means to an end: they were a means to themselves, *and* they produced positive ends.

Fifth, Cal explained, it's critical to take at least one step toward balance and see what happens. Balance means taking one step at a time. One step may be all that you need.

But after a realistic evaluation period, you may find that it is necessary to take a second or third step to experience the reality you seek. Progressively, over time, you can add additional habits as new ones take hold.

This act-observe-evaluate process is effective because it helps us solidify balance gradually. Many people quit balanced behaviors because they try to pack in too many prematurely.

Cal urged Ray to follow this process with just one area of his life. "Once you see the benefits, and balanced behaviors are rooted, then you can replicate the same sequence with another area of life," Cal said.

Ray gave the matter some scrutiny and opted to begin with his health, since so much hinged on it. His poor health was affecting the quality of his work and relationships.

He was excited to give this a try, and he left the café ready for something miraculous.

In reality, he was about to learn how difficult it can be to break the gravitational pull of old habits and truly embrace balance.

6

THAT EVENING AFTER work, Ray rushed home and took out a legal pad. He was so excited that he could barely concentrate.

"Let's see," he contemplated out loud. "What is the first step? Oh, that's right." He remembered that he needed to establish a vision of what he wanted to experience.

That was easy. He wanted to lose fifty pounds.

Hmmm, he thought. *I'm supposed to lose this weight slowly.*

He wrote "lose fifty pounds in one year" on the paper, licking his lips unconsciously as he wrote. He felt that was balanced.

Then he tried to remember the next step. It had something to do with visualizing what balance would look like.

He casually stroked his cheek. Nothing was coming to mind.

"What would balance *look* like?" he asked himself. He didn't have any idea. He just wanted results.

"I don't know," he admitted, trying to figure out what to do next. Eventually, he composed some ideas on diet changes and exercise.

The third step was to identify any resistance he was feeling. "Resistance to what?" he wailed, throwing his hands up in the air.

This was really becoming annoying. It had all made perfect sense this morning, and now it was breaking up in his memory.

He reasoned that perhaps he had no resistance. Maybe he was more balanced than others. He thought that losing fifty pounds in a year was perfectly sensible, so he felt no inner resistance.

That also meant he could skip the fourth step, something about "reframing."

Now he could move right into step five: advancing headlong toward the goal with one new habit!

He liked the idea of walking, so he decided to walk one hour a day. That wasn't too much, considering he used to run for several hours daily. He could walk thirty minutes over lunch and another thirty minutes in the evening.

Over the next week, Ray walked every day and really enjoyed it. He was overjoyed with his new philosophy, as well. Balance was wonderful. He was giving himself a whole year to get results. There was no rush or pressure.

But as time passed, Ray wondered if he was doing this right. Something seemed to be missing. This wasn't nearly as magical as he had envisioned.

Cal had talked about something more grand and elaborate. The people who were coming into the café seemed to be experiencing an amazing transformation.

It could be that balance wasn't as exciting as everyone made it out to be. Maybe, but it still seemed to work for them.

He shrugged and decided he would give it one more month before reporting back to Cal.

After a few weeks, the initial euphoria waned, and he was beginning to question the entire process. He was barely losing any weight, so he doubled his walking time. He dreaded dieting but thought he might have to do this to gain traction.

As he put these measures into effect, he didn't see results, so he seriously entertained extreme measures. Balance didn't seem to have the slightest impact. Yet this also threatened to undermine everything Cal said.

After three weeks, Ray returned to the café disappointed and tired. The only thing keeping him from giving up entirely was curiosity.

He was wondering how the old man would respond to someone who made every reasonable attempt to be balanced but who wasn't getting results.

Cal listened closely to Ray's account and decided the best approach was to walk Ray through the sequence one step at a time, *again*.

First, what did he want to experience?

Ray took out his crumpled paper and read the goal.

Cal stopped him and explained this is not about setting a typical goal. He comforted Ray, suggesting that this is a very common first mistake.

The key is to take time completely out of the picture. A vision is timeless, whereas a goal is time bound. The problem with goals is that they put pressure on people to produce results by a certain arbitrary time.

This produces stress. It also puts the subconscious mind in a position to resent the new behaviors and desire a return to the past.

A vision, on the other hand, is purely experiential. It assumes a new reality is possible and gives us the ability to experience it, conceptually, right now.

Finally, a vision produces tremendous motivation, often more than a goal. A vision stems from a view of the universe that is not fixed and frozen. Instead, it is dynamic and changing. A vision is one of many potential realities. When we realize this for the first time, we may feel like we've just stepped into a new world.

"We've left a world where we think our problems define us, and limitations are permanent," Cal said. "The new world we find ourselves in is a place where one reality is just as possible as another. The first step toward bringing these new realities to life is to *see* them."

Ray blinked, trying to imagine an alternate reality.

"When this occurs, motivation is galvanized automatically, and this helps us catalyze action."

Cal urged Ray to throw the goal away and replace it with a time-less, experiential, vision of health.

Second, Ray needed to figure out "how" this new reality would unfold through balance. A goal might require hours of exercise and stringent dieting, but balance could offer something far more exqui-site. What might that be?

Cal suggested that we look at this from the frame of *cause*. In other words, today we live in a reality that we may not want. The question to ask is, "What is causing it?" When we list the causes, we may be closer to our new reality than we think. The most important step is to find the most potent cause.

Cal said, "If you list all the factors contributing to being over-weight, the primary one is almost always overeating. Excessive eat-ing leads to excess fat.

Balance means bringing diet between the extremes of overeat-ing and starvation into a healthy middle ground. Over time, balance will graciously lower excess weight and keep it at a constant."

Ray wasn't sure this was true. He argued that exercise must have more to do with this than diet alone.

Cal agreed that exercise is important but again challenged Ray to think about this from the perspective of cause.

If we exercise for health benefits, we don't necessarily need to do it to lose weight. Conversely, if we exercise to lose excess weight, this means that our diet has done the damage first. It is therefore the predecessor, the primary cause.

This seemed uncomfortably true. Ray was troubled, though, because this meant he was finally going to have to get his overeating habit in check, and he had no idea how.

This is what step three is for, because what Ray was feeling was actually the natural resistance of the subconscious mind to balance. Ray really believed that balance was unachievable because he didn't think he was capable of eating moderately.

To Ray's surprise, Cal wrote this down on the paper. He congratulated Ray for uncovering the largest impediment to change.

"Ray, you're not overweight because you're averse to dieting or exercise," Cal said. "It's not because you're a lazy person. It's because you don't *believe* you're capable of eating moderately."

This meant the problem was in his mind, not anywhere else. It was not rooted in his body or in the physical world. If Ray could change his mind, he could change his reality. That's why vision is so critical to change because a vision fundamentally rewires our minds.

Cal said that this is where the fourth step comes into play. We can't fool ourselves into believing something—that is why motivational tricks rarely work for long. We might get emotionally pumped up at first, but this feeling dissolves quickly.

The only way to authentically change is from the inside out. This can *only* be done by actually changing the way you see reality. Cal termed this "reframing," as though you are looking at something through a new lens.

He asked Ray to take a step back and examine his belief. "Is it really true that you're incapable of eating moderately? Have you ever actually tried it?"

Ray thought about it. He could have sworn that he had tried moderation many times and failed. As he racked his brains for an example, all he could recall were pop diets or short-term fixes. He'd never modified his eating patterns outside the context of trying to lose weight fast.

Cal said that people who eat moderately rarely do so to reach a goal quickly. As simple as this was, it gave Ray an insight that he never saw before.

This was Ray's "aha" moment. If he took time out of the equation and ate moderately as a life habit, perhaps this would have a material impact.

In fact, this became the first step Ray would take. The results stunned him.

7

BECAUSE RAY'S VISION wasn't limited by time, he found eating in moderation much easier. And he quickly found that wasn't the only reason it seemed effortless.

First, balance meant he could still eat the same foods he enjoyed. Extreme diets usually meant deprivation. Balance, on the other hand, gave him permission to eat savory and flavorful foods but simply in smaller quantities.

Second, balance took away inner resistance to change. Deprivation created a built-in trigger to seek a return to his former habits. Balance gave him enjoyment, so there was nothing for his subconscious mind to resist.

Third, Ray gradually added some healthier choices that he enjoyed. They became pleasing substitutes. For example, he chose herbal teas instead of soft drinks, salads instead of fries and chips, and dark chocolate or nuts instead of other snacks. This helped him feel full naturally while reducing calories painlessly.

The last reason shocked him the most: he discovered that will-power isn't always the culprit for overeating. Actually, high-sugar but low-nutrition foods stimulated unhealthy cravings that were nearly impossible for Ray to curtail.

When Ray brought his diet into balance, a radical change occurred. He lost the dysfunctional cravings automatically. In their place, he experienced natural hunger, natural satiation, and natural fat loss.

He didn't lose fifty pounds overnight. He lost weight imperceptibly over time. In the place of speed and pressure were balanced behaviors that he could enjoy, and maintain with ease. After a few months, he could see and feel a noticeable improvement.

He was a believer in balance, and he wanted to apply the same process to other areas of his life.

After discussing this with Cal, he decided to shift his focus to his career. He disliked his job and felt like he was running on a hamster wheel, going nowhere. How could this process work for his job?

Cal counseled him to walk through the same five-step sequence and come back the next day with some ideas.

At home, Ray took out a piece of paper and began writing enthusiastically. First, he knew that he wanted to actually enjoy his work, and move up the career ladder. This wasn't a goal but a new reality he could envision.

Second, he began thinking about balance. His mind started to go blank again, so he sat up straight in his chair and tried to concentrate. *What would balance look like at work?* he wondered, and his brain began percolating ideas.

Typically, his days were full of meetings and paperwork. He spent too much time in the break room as well. He thought that balance would look like more actual work and fewer meetings and breaks. He wrote this down.

Next, he needed to be aware of his own inner resistance to balance. He sat and waited. After a few minutes, he could only conclude that he felt no inner resistance.

That was when he knew something was going terribly awry. He started doodling on the paper and caught a glimpse of a child throwing a baseball outside his window. Shadows danced and expanded on the floor as dusk darkened the sky. Ray realized he would have to ask Cal for another course correction the following day.

The next morning Ray burst into the café and described his dilemma. Within seconds, Cal saw the roadblock and walked him through the sequence.

"First, you need to create a more compelling vision," Cal said. To do this, Ray needed to elaborate on the benefits: Why enjoy the work? Why get a promotion? What tangible difference would this reality offer over the present one?

"This is the foundation to the other parts of the sequence," Cal explained. "Dwelling on the vision and the benefits you accrue gives you the natural motivation needed to overcome inertia. Unless you feel positive emotions about the vision, you are unlikely to take the next steps toward bringing it to life."

Second, he said that "working harder" or "taking fewer breaks" ignores the most important aspect of change, which is cause.

Cal said, "We must first understand what is causing us to be stuck in our present reality. Normally, imbalance is the cause. To reverse the situation, it's helpful to identify our imbalanced behaviors and determine which are doing the most damage."

Ray still struggled to grasp this. So Cal gave him some instructions: write down every cause, and then rank the causes from lowest to highest in terms of damage. The one that is doing the most harm is the primary contributor to his current reality.

Balance would then be doing the exact opposite of this behavior.

Cal took a sip of coffee and studied Ray's expression, which seemed to be muted. For some reason, it made perfect sense with health, but it just wasn't resonating in terms of career.

The old man took in a deep breath and offered more detail on how balance could work in a job scenario. "Essentially, it's critical to measure the degree to which 'importance' characterizes your daily energy," he said.

"On one end of the spectrum, a person might spend nearly one hundred percent of his or her time on activities that are insignificant. This is obviously an extreme, and the person will most likely not advance."

Cal continued. "The other extreme might be to become a workaholic. You might work on important tasks, but you work around the clock and neglect your health, family, and relationships."

He explained that people who fall into this category often work harder versus smarter and that some have trouble delegating. Over time, quality suffers under swelling fatigue. Eventually the adverse effects of negligence unravel the positive effects of all the hard work.

"That's why balance is really the only sane option. It's the comfortable middle point between these two polarities. You focus on doing what is most important for your employer," Cal concluded.

Ray experienced a sudden moment of insight. Everything seemed to make sense and come to life. He left the café excited and went to work on crafting his new vision.

He knew that he was capable of more, but he had stayed largely in the shadows. He was aware of opportunities that could be of great value to the company's clients and generate revenue. However, he had avoided them because he knew there would be challenges and potential rejection. It was easier to play it safe.

Armed with this new awareness, he tore up the old paper and started again. What was the vision he wanted to experience? If he was honest, he longed for a new reality where he was engaged in meaningful work, using his strengths, and putting himself into a position of upward mobility.

To achieve this, he would undoubtedly have to leave his comfort zone. This meant researching and presenting ideas and working in new ways.

When he wrote this down, the inner resistance was palpable. Like turning a faucet, the fears came flowing out freely: *What if I fail? I might appear ridiculous. I might work hard and still end up in the same spot.*

He wondered, after writing these objections, if he was capable of "reframing" them. After all, he really did hold these perspectives inside.

He thought about each of them carefully. He realized failure or looking ridiculous were possibilities, but he *already* appeared ridiculous to many, so what could he lose? *If I take action, I'm at least more likely to succeed than if I stay stranded in my comfort zone.*

But what scared him the most was churning out more effort with no guarantee of success. As he reflected on his life, he could see a pattern that ran throughout numerous broken relationships and job failures.

The pattern was doomsday thinking, which was inherently fatalistic and created a self-fulfilling prophesy. Ray habitually held back, hoping others would take the first step and bear the risk. When they didn't, he retreated further, and others regarded him as a passive recluse.

To break the cycle, he knew he needed to do the exact opposite. Specifically, he would take the first step in making some of these potential projects real, regardless of his trepidation.

Before long, he no longer recognized himself or his job.

8

RAY'S CAREER TOOK on an entirely new sheen the minute he created his vision. He brought contagious energy into his work and actively embraced a number of key initiatives. His manager, and others, took notice. They wondered what had happened.

In some cases, they were also disappointed. The old Ray, who took on any menial project, suddenly began saying no. Now he was busy with larger, more important deliverables and had to strategically prioritize his activities.

He also became a more capable communicator and delegator. In a short time, his manager gave him a promotion.

Ray's life was really taking shape. As he became busier, he frequented the café less often. Occasionally he'd pop in and recount his successes with Cal.

One day, he thought he would try the same process for his sagging relationship with Jenny. In his mind, this area was hopeless. As he was familiar with the sequence, he didn't need to review it with Cal. However, he did want to know what balance might look like with relationships.

Cal's approach caught Ray completely by surprise. He offered little commentary on being less argumentative, diffusing conflict, or being a better listener. He said the issue revolved around one word: relate.

"The root word of 'relationship' is 'relate,'" Cal said. "Most of us spend time with others, but few of us genuinely relate to others. Relating is a bigger concept than listening."

"Many people communicate verbally, but that's not necessarily relating," he continued. "They may be articulate, intelligent, and eloquent but show no concern about others at all. Balance is finding that middle ground between listening and communicating, so you can clear the way to an authentic relationship."

This insight hit Ray like a punch in the gut. He knew that he had lost his ability to genuinely relate to Jenny; all his energy was consumed in getting her to relate to him.

He knew exactly what he needed to do and bid Cal good-bye. But before Ray could leave, Cal put his arm out to stop him.

"Wait," he called out. "There's something you need to know about balance that we haven't discussed yet!"

Ray didn't have time to listen. He was too busy making positive changes and hustled to his car.

As Ray practiced relating with Jenny, their dynamic completely improved. Old irritations dissolved as he took on a genuine appreciation for her. Similarly, as he changed toward her, she reciprocated. This brought the relationship to such an amicable place that they started to plan for the wedding.

It was a miracle. Ray was euphoric and a firm believer in balance.

Now, with even more on his plate, he had less time to go to the café. One day, before an important meeting, Ray hurried in to give Cal the good news about his relationship.

Cal seemed pleased but tried to press him on something. He kept trying to give Ray some final perspective on balance.

"Listen," Ray said. "I couldn't be happier and really don't see the need to go into any more theoretical musing. As a matter of fact, I better get going. Today's a busy day!"

It was as if life had suddenly worked for Ray after decades of frustration. What on earth could be troubling Cal, pushing him to talk about a final principle? Couldn't the old man just be happy for him without complicating matters?

Ray was so full of life and energy that he felt invincible. He doubled his exercise schedule and began working later at nights. He believed that he could grow all his results and that this would lead to an even better life.

He began applying his project management training to the wedding preparations, creating schedules and hiring people to assist Jenny and her mother.

Before long, all of Ray's progress began to disappear. He started eating more, sleeping less, and cutting out his exercise to make more time for work. He and Jenny began arguing, especially as he micromanaged every aspect of their plans. He gained weight, and old health problems reappeared.

What is happening? Ray wondered. How could all his success leave him so fast?

Even his work began to suffer as he made some poor decisions and overreacted to his colleagues. His boss suggested he take some time off to "recharge."

After work, still fuming over what his boss had said, he got into a yelling match with Jenny, and she threatened to call off the engagement.

That night, he sat staring at the TV, paralyzed by shock. Everything was going down the tube. Why? He had followed Cal's advice and experienced an irrevocable turnaround. Now it was as if he had never approached him in the café all those months ago.

Ray gazed at the TV screen, defocusing his eyes so the image was distorted. The words sounded jumbled and far away. The air conditioning kicked on, and he felt a gentle breeze whirling out of the vent.

Something a man said caught his attention, and Ray snapped into focus. It was an interview, and a CEO was talking about reengineering a bankrupt enterprise.

"I inherited a business with a strong sales force, but our product and service models weren't up to snuff," the CEO told the host. "The guy before me felt the imbalance could be offset by aggressive advertising and sales tactics. Unfortunately," he continued, "market disillusionment eventually cannibalized sales efforts. We went into bankruptcy."

That new CEO had been faced with an uphill battle and a challenge that industry analysts considered impossible. Yet he'd managed to reverse the trend by bringing products and operations into a commensurate stature with sales.

"Each of these parts of the business needed to be balanced," he said.

Then the CEO added something that jarred Ray and made him sit up on his oversized couch: "A business is an interdependent system. Each unit needs to be maximized by balance," he said. "When you do this, not only does the unit itself improve, but all other units improve as well. When you improve all units simultaneously, you can get exponential benefits across the board. That's when our business really started to take off," he explained. "Greater balance produces greater results."

The lightbulb in Ray's mind clicked on at that moment, and he snapped his fingers. That must have been exactly what Cal had been trying to say. As long as he brought each part of his life into balance, all the other parts began benefiting as well.

He looked back and recalled how his health had improved and how it had had a positive impact on his work and relationships—almost by osmosis.

As his work improved, it created less stress. This created a spillover effect on his health and relationships.

As he worked on his relationships, he experienced greater overall health, and more productivity at work.

So what happened? What brought all this crashing down?

He knew what the answer was: ego. At some point, Ray fell into the trap of believing that all this was happening because of his power.

He believed that he could circumvent the laws of nature and bypass balance. The minute this happened, all the aspects of his life that had improved through balance began to atrophy through imbalance.

"Greater balance, greater reward," he repeated aloud.

9

RAY ADOPTED ALL the principles of balance for each area of his life again. Within weeks, his body felt better, and he gained more energy and alertness.

He mended relationships at work and brought his job back into balance. He apologized to Jenny and stopped trying to manipulate the wedding preparations.

Greater balance did indeed create greater results. He was eager to share this discovery with Cal and began going back to the café. Cal was never there, though.

At first, Ray figured he was probably just missing him. It wasn't like Cal lived there. He had a life outside of helping others. Didn't he? After a while, he asked people at the café, but nobody had seen the old man for months. Was he on vacation? Was he ill?

Soon, Ray and Jenny were married and left on their honeymoon. It was a wonderful time, and Ray was excited to share this and other events with Cal.

When they arrived back home, Ray returned to the café several times but still couldn't find his friend. Now he was really concerned. How could he find him? He didn't even know his last name.

That evening he was sitting in his study, and something caught his eye. It was a familiar business card buried beneath a heap of paperclips. He snatched it off the table, suddenly remembering that Cal had given it to him during one of their first sessions.

He picked up the phone and anxiously dialed the number. His heart pounded with anticipation. He felt like it would literally leap out of his chest.

The phone rang a few times, and someone picked up on the other end. Ray's blood pressure shot into fifth gear.

A thin, distant voice crackled, "Hello?" It sounded like a very frail woman.

"Yes." Ray could barely hide his worry. "May I speak with Cal?"

He was greeted by a labored pause. "Who is this?"

Ray explained who he was and insisted that Cal knew him.

"Oh, you're one of the people from the café," she said and paused for a moment. "I'm Cal's wife, Jane. Cal passed away a few weeks ago. I'm sorry, dear."

Ray felt like he had suddenly fallen through a trapdoor and was submerged in a vat of ice water.

He tried desperately to hold back the tears. "I'm so sorry, Jane. What happened?"

She recounted how Cal had fallen and then faded after a few weeks in the hospital. As she recited the grim details, Ray let his head fall back and closed his eyes.

His mouth was dry, and he suddenly had difficulty swallowing. The realization that he was never going to see Cal again began to sink deep into his stomach.

"Don't feel too bad, Ray. He led a good life. Ninety years is a long time for this world."

"What?" Ray stood up in surprise. "Did you say he was ninety?"

He had thought Cal was in his seventies!

Then he heard papers shuffling on the other end of the phone.

"What did you say your name was again?" she asked.

"Ray."

She seemed to be looking for something. He heard a drawer rolling on its wheels and a metal door slam shut.

"Oh yes, here it is."

She told him that Cal had written him a letter in case he called, as he had done with other people from the café.

She opened the envelope and read it. Ray pressed the receiver against his head so firmly that his ear ached from the pressure.

Dear Ray, I hoped you would call so you could receive this last secret of balance.

Many people realize that balance in one area can produce balance in other areas of life.

However, they don't realize the power of bringing all the areas of your life into balance at once.

Strive to do this, Ray, and you will learn the greatest secret: Greater balance, greater reward.

P.S. Please take my seat at the café, and teach this secret to others.

When Jane finished, Ray quietly thanked her and ended the phone call. Over the next hour, he contemplated Cal's parting words.

10

ANGELA SAT IN the café, her body numb after another sleepless night. The breakup with Jim was yet one more lost battle in a long succession of skirmishes.

Why were her friends getting married, having children, and enjoying their lives while she remained forever trapped in a revolving door? She tried everything. She saw psychologists, psychiatrists, coaches, and read every book she could find on relationships. Unfortunately, nothing seemed to stick. Some puzzle piece was missing.

Like a chain reaction, every area in her life seemed to ricochet out of control. Her work was suffering, as she had difficulty concentrating, and the doctor said her health was beginning to decline.

As she cogitated over her problems, she noticed another person at a table with a strange old man. He always sat in the back corner of the restaurant and seemed to attract bystanders like a human magnet.

It became so predictable you could say it was almost annoying. People would casually strike up a conversation with him. Next, they sat with him, telling him everything about their lives. Eventually, they stopped coming, and a new wave of people took their place. The cycle seemed eternal.

Was he a psychologist, a guru, or maybe a financial planner? Perhaps he ran some kind of Ponzi scheme.

It frustrated her because the more people talked with him, the more they appeared to undergo a metamorphosis. It was as if he had given them a makeover.

She heard a siren outside and turned abruptly, accidentally toppling her mug over. Hot coffee spilled across the table, and she cursed under her breath.

A large, friendly lady behind the counter walked over with a wet rag. She efficiently wiped the surface of the table then eyed something amiss in the pantry and turned away. At that moment, a middle-aged man stood up and affectionately grasped the old man's hand.

"Oh brother," Angela scoffed, unconsciously rolling her eyes.

The buckled wood planks shook beneath Angela's feet as the man strolled briskly past her, and she lifted her index finger to get his attention.

"What's going on with that old man?" she asked pointedly. After years of watching this peculiar scene, she was going to get to the bottom of it.

The man was obviously in a hurry and couldn't speak long. "He's some retired executive. I don't know from where. He helps people through some kind of philosophy of the mind. You know?"

"Yeah, I bet," Angela said with a hint of sarcasm roughly the size of a boulder.

"You should talk with him," the man responded and then left. The old shutters barely clung to the window as the door slammed shut.

"This place is ancient," Angela sniffed, glancing at the wood beams on the ceiling and the rusty metal tins lined up on the shelves. It seemed like a time capsule, something petrified from the past.

It was time to go to work, but a mysterious force weighed heavy on her shoulders. *Goodness, I have to get more sleep*, she thought. Her legs felt like they were clasped in iron.

It made her stop. She slowly turned toward the back of the café. It was time. She decided to go see the man at last. It couldn't hurt. He was probably a charlatan, but he did seem to have a magnetic con-nection with people.

As she neared his table, she was struck by how small he was. In her mind, she had built him up to be a giant.

However, the minute he looked up, he exuded an unmistakable energy. He turned to her and smiled.

Angela gulped. What was she doing, speaking to some strange old man she didn't know? Yet, in some unexplainable way, he seemed familiar.

"Hello, my name is Ray," he said.

Angela's life was about to change in a way she never expected.

Summary

AFTER READING THIS story, many people have told me they really enjoyed it and certainly have a fresh perspective on balance. However, they're still not 100 percent sure how to "put the pieces together."

Therefore, I'd like to offer a summary of what the book teaches and then how to create your own "aha" moment.

1. Balance is power.

The entire book can be boiled down to a single perspective: balance has a radically underappreciated power to transform your life and reverse common—even universal—problems.

Consider the challenge I experienced with weight loss, which I touched on at the beginning of the book: I was hefting around an extra fifty pounds before the age of thirty.

What I didn't mention was the fact that I had spent the previous ten years trying nearly every popular diet and exercise program on the market. None of these worked for long. After the initial euphoria of a shiny, new approach wore off, I found myself looking for something else. Even when I succeeded, I soon reverted to old habits.

Something seemed to be tugging me back to this old, familiar problem, like an unexplained gravitational pull.

This changed when I encountered that mystical vision while walking in the park. Essentially, I realized the next point about balance.

2. Sometimes life is like a coin: our solutions are the flip side of our problems.

As I walked, it dawned on me that I was looking for answers so desperately that I missed the obvious.

I didn't need to go out and "find" the answer. All I needed was to "see" what was *causing* my problem in the first place. When I accepted the root cause of the problem, and started to bring balance into this part of my life, my situation normalized automatically.

After a few months, the weight melted off.

What is so fascinating is that I didn't need iron willpower. It seemed effortless, especially after a few days of readjusting to some new eating habits. I lost the weight and exercised a fraction of the time I used to. Also, I began to experience better health and physical vitality!

Sound impossible? It's really not, as seen in the next point.

3. Balance works because of natural laws, not because of our great effort, time, and ingenuity.

This is good news because you don't need to supply the power of transformation. Balance will do this for you.

Instead, you simply need to be able to discern natural laws that operate in the systems that we live in.

Quite frankly, the primary requirement is humility. You just need to be open to what the answer is and accept it.

If it's this easy, why doesn't everyone follow balance? The answer may surprise you.

4. Balance is one of the most misunderstood principles in the world.

When you think about it, a surreal contradiction takes place with what people say and believe about balance. For example, if you ask people about balance, they'll almost always say they believe in it. They may even say its value is "self-evident" or "incontrovertible."

Yet if you look at their behavior, you'll often see just the opposite. For instance, if you ask about a "balanced diet," most people will agree this is the "obvious" way to eat. However, few actually practice this. The same identical phenomenon occurs with finances and work-life balance.

Have you noticed this, too?

People say that they *should* balance their budget or live within their means, but do they actually do this?

Likewise, people almost unanimously assert the importance of balancing work and personal demands. Yet the sad reality is that so many people sacrifice the things money can't buy (like health and relationships) in favor of career demands.

What on earth is happening? Why are people living in this dichotomy?

5. We can't escape from the prison we don't know we're in.
The reason for this odd phenomenon is actually quite simple: people are not *really* sure that balance is the answer.

If you want to know what people really believe, just observe behavior. The truth always reveals itself in action. People may *say* they believe in balance, but—in fact—they usually harbor some suspicion and resistance.

Why do you think people resist balance?

As I've discussed this with readers, one key force that surfaces is culture. Let me illustrate.

We live in the "modern age." In this age, how do we solve some of our biggest problems? Well, we do so through science and technology. As a result, we can drive and fly, eradicate illnesses, and connect with anyone online. On one hand, there is great value in our technological progress.

However, how might this progress subconsciously have an impact on our perceptions about balance? The answer is that, for many of us, we truly believe that we should be able to solve virtually any problem if we just throw enough money and technology at it.

There should be a product to solve every problem. Can't we just push a button and alter our reality?

Subtly, over time, we've come to believe that balance is old-fashioned, boring, or powerless. When I used to think about balance, I nearly burst out laughing; I thought that it was some antiquated advice my grandmother might give. *Why would I want to mess around with balance for my health when I can throw new exercise equipment, gym memberships, and exciting diets at the problem?*

Can you relate to this kind of thinking? If so, you're among the majority of people I've talked with. And this is precisely where our resistance to balance is coming from.

As a result of this perspective, we're in a prison that we're most likely *unaware* of... the prison of unconsciously resisting the very thing that can free us from our challenges: balance!

Now, how can we change this?

6. We can escape from our limitations once we've discovered where they are coming from.

You can't trick yourself into believing something you don't. This is why positive thinking and other motivational ploys often fail. Transformation occurs when you see the truth, which is often hidden within a lie.

The *Greater Balance, Greater Reward* method of self-questioning helps us peel the onion back, layer by layer, until we expose a fallacy in our thinking.

For my weight and health problems, the truth became apparent when I started to question how well our modern remedies were really working. Think about it: have new exercise equipment, gym memberships, and diets *really* solved the problem that so many people are having with their health?

Sometimes they do. But in many cases they haven't, and for many, the problem is actually getting worse—with people of all ages!

Now take a step further, and apply this same questioning with other problems we face.

Have technology and innovation *really* made our lives easier, given us more free time, or reduced stress? It's interesting that people once thought machines would replace domestic chores and computers would reduce workload in our careers.

The paradox is that this is true, yet, on the other hand, the world we all experience is actually becoming more stressful and complex by the minute. Many of us are literally drowning in the minutia of day-to-day life while watching the things that matter most suffer.

So what are we missing?

Personally, I think we're overlooking something that's timeless and universal. However, it can't be bought, sold, or manufactured on an assembly line.

The answer is balance. When we put balance to work in each area of our lives, we truly experience greater balance, *greater* reward.

So how do we put balance to work?

7. Balance works best when you remove time from the equation.

What shocked me the most about my "aha" moment with weight loss wasn't how amazing the results were ... but how timeless they seemed.

Instead of setting goals, and feverishly monitoring progress against an arbitrary deadline, I created a timeless vision of my new life.

Then I took just a few practical steps to bring balance into my lifestyle. After a few months, the results were shocking! And it seemed to happen faster than I ever imagined possible.

If this sounds hard to believe, let me share *another* situation where the same type of timeless transformation occurred: this book!

After renewing my health, I tried writing a book about my experience. However, for years I was unable to write clearly and often struggled with "writer's block."

Just when I was ready to give up, I wondered if I could clone the same process I used to lose weight for other problems ... such as writing more productively!

Like a scientist, I dissected my weight loss experience and discovered that it was a five step system that could probably reverse other problems, too!

Believe it or not, I went through all five steps and discovered a glut of internal resistance to writing that I never knew existed.

I wasn't struggling with a lack of writing ability or motivation; the problem was that I was in a prison of my own beliefs, which was blocking progress.

Here are just a few of those beliefs: *I'm not a writer or an author. Nobody will want to read this. I don't know anything about diet or health. I'll probably fail.*

As you can imagine, it's nearly impossible to write when you hold these beliefs as true. But they're not true, and when I really questioned them, I realized I did have something valuable to share.

This process of dissolving inaccurate beliefs liberated me from writer's block almost instantly. Years of "beating my head against the wall" finally ended.

Then I suddenly visualized the book you are reading as a completed work. In my "mind's eye," the book was just as palpable as the image of rejuvenated health that I saw in the park ten years ago.

When I put pen to paper, the book seemed to write itself—and it only took three days!

And the paradox was that I never set out to write the book so quickly. Yet, by creating a clear and compelling vision of the book, I was able to write it faster ... and better ... than ever before!

Can you see why I not only want to share this process with you but am actually *compelled* to write about it? I know firsthand just how powerful this process is, and I want you to experience it for yourself.

Are you ready?

Your "Aha" Moment

AT THIS POINT, you've read about my "aha" moment and the fictitious account of Ray. Now it's your turn to create greater balance in your life!

Readers have told me that they, too, feel just as excited as I am about balance once they understand the mechanics—but they need a road map.

The best path to follow is the same one that Cal gave Ray in chapter 5:

> *Step 1: Pick an area of life you would like to improve, and see the improvement as if it is already a present reality.*
> *Step 2: Determine what balance would look like, as if it's already being practiced in this area of your life.*
> *Step 3: Pay attention to inner resistance to balance from your subconscious mind.*
> *Step 4: Reframe your thinking by questioning your own assumptions in light of objective reality.*
> *Step 5: Take just one step toward balance, and see what happens.*

As you follow this process, don't rush. Take time to absorb these questions, and think about them deeply.

Then, pick an area of your life that you would like to improve, and follow the process step by step.

Remember to take time out of the equation, because an unhealthy preoccupation with time only creates stress. The changes you seek will come in their own good time as you apply the steps conscientiously.

Finally, I would like to offer you a gift just for reading this book: my *Greater Balance Action Guide*. It's a downloadable form that simulates some of the questions that Cal uses to guide Ray through his transformation. If you get stuck or have trouble in a certain stage, this tool gently helps coax you forward.

Best of success in your journey into greater balance, *greater* reward!

Download Your *Free* Audiobook and Action Guide Now.

Many readers have experienced greater success by downloading the Greater Balance Audiobook and Action Guide.

To download, visit **www.greaterbalancebook.com**.

Your Input Is Welcome

THANK YOU FOR reading this book! Your feedback is welcome, and will also help make updated versions even better.

To this end, please take a moment to post your review on Amazon. A million thanks in advance!

—Jeff Kooz, Author, Musician, and Modern-Day Philosopher

To obtain information on Jeff's books, music, and Webinars visit: www.meet-jeff-kooz.com

Enjoy Kooz Quips

BRING THE POWER of balance into your life with one inspirational quote per week!

Kooz Quips are pointers to the book's most important messages.

To read a few quips, and start receiving these right away, visit **www.koozquips.com**.

Made in the USA
Middletown, DE
22 February 2017